FINDING CALM IN THE STORM

Healing the anxious young woman,
finding your inner peace, surrendering in the words

DIANE SHIREWOOD

Table of Contents

"Finding Calm in the Storm"

When life gets tough, and the winds start to blow

And the storm clouds gather, dark and low

It is so easy to feel overwhelmed, and out of control

And it is hard to find calm, in a world that's so full

But amidst the chaos, there's a stillness within

And a place of peace, that we can tap into, like a win

It's a place of calm, that's deep within our soul

And it's a place of refuge, that can make us whole

Finding calm in the storm, is not always easy

And it takes practice, and patience, and being breezy

It's about learning to breathe, and letting go of fear

And it's about trusting ourselves, and our inner seer

It's about finding the beauty, in the midst of the storm

And seeing the light, even when it seems forlorn

It's about focusing on what we can control
And letting go of the rest, that's not our goal

It's about finding the support, that we need to thrive
And reaching out for help, when we need to arrive
It's about being kind, to ourselves and to others
And finding the courage, to stand up for our own
druthers

In the midst of chaos, when the winds of change blow
strong
And the raging storms of life seem to last so long
It can be hard to find a peaceful place to be
To find some calm in the storm, and let your spirit free

But even in the darkest hour, there is a light
A shining beacon, that can guide you through the night
It is the stillness that resides within your heart
The calm that comes when you let go and do your part

For the storm may rage around you, and the thunder roll
But deep within your soul, there is a quiet hole
A space that is untouched by the raging winds
A place where you can find the peace that begins

It's not easy to find this space, to find this peace
To let go of the fear and let the tension release
But if you take a moment to sit and breathe
You'll find that your mind begins to ease

Focus on your breath, and let the thoughts just be
And soon you'll find that your mind begins to see
The beauty that is all around you, even in the storm
And the calmness that you've been searching for, begins to form

For it's in the midst of chaos, that we can learn to grow
To find the strength to face our fears, and let them go
To trust in the power that resides within our hearts
To let our light shine, and play our unique part

So let the storm rage on, and let the winds blow strong

For deep within your soul, there is a peaceful song

A melody that is waiting to be heard

A light that is waiting to be shared with the world

Let us find calm, in the midst of the storm

And let us trust ourselves, to weather it like a norm

For in the end, we will emerge stronger than before

And we will find peace, that's worth so much more

"Dear Young Women"

Dear young woman, I write to you today

To offer guidance on your life's pathway

You are a precious gem, so bright and bold

With a heart full of love, and a spirit that's gold

In a world that can be tough and cruel

Hold onto your dreams, don't play the fool

Believe in yourself, trust your intuition

And don't let anyone hold you back from your mission

You are capable of amazing things

A powerful force with the potential to spread your wings

Embrace your unique qualities, let them shine

And let your light radiate, so others may find

Your beauty is more than skin deep

It comes from within, it's yours to keep

Be proud of who you are, embrace your flaws

And know that perfection is not the cause

You may face obstacles, hurdles to overcome

But with perseverance, they will come undone

Remember, each failure is a lesson learned

An opportunity for growth, a new way to turn

Surround yourself with people who inspire

Those who lift you up and help you aspire

Let go of those who bring you down

And don't let anyone steal your crown

Find your passion, chase your dreams

Let them guide you like a flowing stream

Take risks, be bold, and don't be afraid

Of the unknown or the price to be paid

Be kind, be compassionate, show empathy

For everyone, regardless of their identity

Stand up for what's right, speak out for justice

And never be afraid to express your kindness

Know that you are loved, you are enough
A shining star with the world in your cuff
And when you feel lost, remember this truth
That your inner light will guide you through

Dear young woman, embrace your power
You have the ability to make the world better
With your heart full of love and your spirit strong
You can do anything, your life can be a beautiful song

"Rising Above the Storm"

When the storm clouds gather and the winds blow
strong
And the rain pours down, heavy and long
We may feel lost, alone and afraid
As we struggle to find our footing in the cascade

But in the midst of the storm, there's a strength that
lies
A power within us, that helps us rise
It's the courage that comes from deep inside
The resilience that helps us to abide

For we are stronger than we think
And we can rise above the storm, and never sink
We can stand tall, and face the winds head-on
And find the strength to carry on

It's in the struggles that we grow

And it's through the challenges that we know

That we have the power to overcome

And to rise above, under the sun

So let us embrace the storm, and all its might

And let us hold on to hope, and not lose sight

For in the end, we will find our way

And we will rise above, day by day

We will emerge stronger, wiser, and more whole

And we will find the courage to reach our goal

For we are warriors, fierce and true

And we can rise above, no matter what we go through

Let us rise above the storm, with strength and grace

And let us keep moving forward, at our own pace

For in the end, we will find our peace

And our light will shine, and never cease

"Embracing Your Inner Strength"

Within you lies a force so great

A strength that knows no bounds

A power born of love and grace

That lifts you up when you feel down

Embrace your inner warrior's might

And all that makes you who you are

Let your courage guide you right

And shine your light like a bright star

In the depths of your being lies

A power beyond compare

A strength that knows no compromise

And a light that always dares

Embrace your inner strength with pride

And let it be your guide

Stand tall in all that you believe

And let your spirit rise

For in the power of your soul

Lies the strength to conquer all

To overcome the doubts and fears

And rise to every call

Embrace the warrior within

And let your light shine bright

For you are capable of anything

With your inner strength and might

Let your courage be your armor

And your love your sword and shield

Embrace your inner warrior's might

And let your true self be revealed

"Listen to your Heart"

Listen to your heart, the whispers that it speaks

For it holds the key to all that you seek

It knows your deepest desires, your hopes and your
dreams

And it will guide you towards your chosen themes

In a world that's ever-changing, and sometimes feels
so cold

Your heart can be your compass, to help you be bold

It will lead you on a journey, through the ups and the
downs

And it will always be there, to lift you up when you're
down

Your heart is a source of power, that lies deep within

And when you learn to listen, you'll find peace within

It will show you the way, to your innermost truth

And it will help you to unleash, your boundless youth

Sometimes the path may be unclear, and the road may seem long

But trust in your heart, and keep moving along

For every step you take, will bring you closer to your goal

And you'll find the strength to carry on, even when it gets tough and droll

Follow your heart, and let it be your guide

And you'll find the courage to face all that you must abide

For in the depths of your soul, lies all that you require

To live a life of purpose, joy, and unbridled fire

Listen to your heart, and embrace all that you are

And you'll shine like the brightest star, from near or far

For when you learn to listen, to the whispers that it speaks

You'll find the truest version of yourself, and all that it seeks

"Breathing Through Life"

Keep breathing, my dear

For life can be a tumultuous ride

And the journey can leave us feeling lost and unclear

But the rhythm of your breath can be your guide

In the moments of chaos and confusion

When you feel like you're drowning in the sea of

emotion

Focus on the sensation of the air rushing in

And the relief of the air flowing out, with each

exhalation

Let the breath be your anchor, your support

The foundation upon which you can build your fort

For the breath is always there, constant and true

A faithful companion to carry you through

Breathe in the calm, let it expand

Throughout your body, let it take command

Feel the tension and stress melting away

As you focus on the present, and let go of the fray

Breathe in the peace, let it fill your soul

Allow it to heal any wound that takes its toll

The breath can be a source of renewal and strength

And with it, you can rise above any length

With each inhalation, let your heart fill with light

And with each exhalation, release what does not feel
right

Breathe in love, breathe out fear

Embrace the hope that is always near

The breath can be a tool for transformation

A way to change your thoughts and alter your vibration

With every breath, you can create a new reality

One that is filled with joy, love, and possibility

So keep breathing, my dear

For in each breath lies a world of promise and cheer

The rhythm of your breath is the rhythm of life

And with it, you can overcome any strife

"Finding Calm in Chaos"

Amidst the storm, a peaceful calm

A beacon of light to guide us home

When the winds of change do blow

And chaos reigns, let go the woe

In the eyes of the hurricane

A stillness found, a welcome refrain

A quietude that soothes the soul

And brings us back to our true goal

In the midst of all the noise

A refuge found, a place of poise

A sanctuary for our minds

And a respite from the daily grind

Take a moment to be still

And let the calmness work its will

Breathe in the stillness deep within

And let the healing light shine in

In the midst of all the tumult
A center found, a peaceful result
A wisdom born of inner grace
That lifts us up and fills our space

In the midst of all the chaos
A hope found, a seed that grows
A faith in all that's yet to be
And the power to set us free

When the storms of life do blow
And chaos reigns, let go the woe
Remember that within us all
Lies the calmness to break the thrall

In the eye of the hurricane
A stillness found, a welcome refrain
A quietude that soothes the soul
And brings us back to our true goal

"The Beauty Within"

Beyond the surface, beyond the skin

Lies a beauty that's found within

A light that shines with gentle grace

And reflects the kindness of the face

For beauty's not just in the eyes

It's in the heart where it resides

It's in the kindness that we share

And in the love that we declare

True beauty comes from deep inside

And is not measured by the tide

It's in the laughter that we find

And in the moments that are kind

It's in the way we treat ourselves

And in the way we treat our friends

It's in the way we lend a hand

And in the way we make amends

Let us celebrate the beauty within
And let it shine through thick and thin
For it's the light that guides us true
And helps us see the beauty in you

Let us cherish the heart that beats
And the love that's found in our deeds
For it's the beauty that we share
That makes life worth living, that we declare

Let your beauty shine bright and true
And embrace the light that's inside of you
For you are a masterpiece of grace
And your beauty shines on in every place

"The Healing Breath"

Breathe in slowly, deeply, and long

Let the air fill your lungs like a soothing song

Breathe out slowly, calmly, and strong

Feel the tension leaving, and the calmness come along

Inhale the light, and exhale the dark

Allow the rhythm of your breath to make its mark

With each inhalation, feel the air energize

And with each exhalation, feel yourself harmonize

Breathe in peace, and breathe out fear

Allow the breath to dry up any tear

Let it fill you with calmness and grace

And guide you towards a happier place

Breathe in hope, and breathe out doubt

Allow the breath to take you on a new route

Let it cleanse you of all that is negative

And fill you with all that is positive

Breathe in love, and breathe out pain
Allow the breath to heal you, again and again
Let it remind you of all that is good
And carry you through any trial that you should

With each inhalation, let your heart open wide
And with each exhalation, feel yourself come alive
Breathe in slowly, deeply, and long
And let the rhythm of your breath be your guide

For breathing is a gift, that we should cherish every day
And the power of your breath can light up any pathway
So breathe in peace, and breathe out stress
And let the rhythm of your breath guide you towards
happiness

These techniques may be simple, but they hold
immense power

To calm the mind, and ease the anxieties that we cower

So practice them often, and with great care

And let the healing power of your breath take you anywhere

"Overcoming Panic Attacks"

Panic attacks, they come out of the blue

A storm of emotions, that we don't know how to

subdue

Our hearts race, our breaths become shallow

And our minds fill with fear, that we can't seem to

swallow

The world around us, starts to spin and whirl

And we feel like we're trapped, in an endless swirl

We try to control, the rising tide of panic

But it's like trying to stop a hurricane, with a mere

picnic

Our thoughts race, and we can't seem to stop

As our worries and fears, rise to the top

We feel like we're drowning, in a sea of anxiety

And we can't find a way out, of this calamity

But there is hope, for those who suffer

From panic attacks, that leave them in a buffer

It starts with acceptance, of what's happening now

And allowing ourselves, to feel without a how

We can try breathing exercises, slow and deep

To calm our mind, and help us keep

Focused on the present, and what's real

Not the fears and worries, that we often feel

Or we can try, a technique called exposure

To face our fears, and gain composure

To gradually confront, what we fear the most

And prove to ourselves, that we can host

And when we feel, like we can't cope alone

We can reach out, for support and a safety zone

To friends, family, or a professional therapist

Who can help us find, a path to persist

With time and effort, we can overcome

These panic attacks, that leave us numb

We can find our way back, to a life that's bright

And let go of the fear, that haunts us at night

If you're struggling, with a panic attack

Remember that there's hope, and a way to get back

To a life that's free, from constant fear and dread

And embrace a future, where you're happy instead

"It's Not Your Fault"

It's easy to blame yourself, when things go wrong

To think that you're the cause, that you don't belong

To carry the weight, of the world on your shoulders

And believe that your mistakes, have made you a

beholder

But hear me now, and hear me clear

It's not your fault, for things you couldn't steer

Life can be unpredictable, and it can throw us

curveballs

And sometimes the weight, of our burdens seems tall

It's not your fault, if you were dealt a difficult hand

Or if you didn't know, how to take a stand

It's not your fault, if you fell down along the way

Or if you had to navigate, through the darkness and

the gray

You are not defined, by your mistakes or your past

And you don't have to carry, the weight that they cast

You can rise above, and find your inner light

And know that you are worthy, and you are enough in sight

It's not your fault, if you've been hurt or betrayed

Or if you've had to walk, a path that was frayed

You can release the guilt, and the shame that you hold

And know that you are strong, and you'll weather the cold

So let go of the blame, and the self-doubt that you feel

And know that you're capable, of healing and of zeal

You can find your inner peace, and your sense of self

And let go of the burden, that you've carried like a shelf

It's not your fault, my dear, for the things that you can't control

And you can find your way forward, and let your spirit
roll
You are worthy, and you are loved, just as you are
And you don't have to carry, the weight that's left you
scarred

So let this be a reminder, when you feel the guilt and
pain
That it's not your fault, and you don't have to carry
that chain
You can let go, and find your way towards the light
And know that you're deserving, of love and a new
sight

"Healing Together"

You and me, two hearts on a quest

To find the peace we both need and the rest

A journey towards healing, towards the light

Together we'll make it, with all our might

We hold each other's hands, through the pain

Together we'll weather every storm and rain

We're not alone, we have each other

Our love will guide us, like a gentle mother

In the depths of our souls, lies the wounds

That have left us scarred, with feelings that cocoon

But we're not defined by our past, by our fears

Together we'll overcome them, wipe away the tears

We'll take each step with grace and love

With each other, we'll rise above

We'll turn our wounds into lessons

Our healing journey, a story of blessings

We'll learn to let go of the past
And focus on the present, where our love will last
We'll cultivate a positive mindset
And find the joy in every aspect

We'll nourish our bodies and souls
With self-care practices, that make us feel whole
We'll breathe in calmness, and let go of stress
Our love will be a beacon, that we both bless

We'll learn to forgive ourselves and others
Our love will grow stronger, like a band of brothers
We'll embrace our vulnerabilities, with open hearts
Our healing journey, a beautiful work of art

You and me, two hearts on a quest
To find healing, to find the rest
Together we'll make it, with love and care
Our journey towards healing, a story to share

"Self-Love"

Self-love is a journey worth taking

A path to inner peace, a road worth making

For when we love ourselves, we shine bright

And everything around us feels just right

It's about embracing who we are, flaws and all

And accepting ourselves, standing tall

It's about honoring our needs and our dreams

And treating ourselves with kindness and esteem

Self-love is not about being selfish or vain

It's about being authentic, true and humane

It's about knowing our worth and our value

And showing ourselves grace, patience and virtue

It's about setting healthy boundaries and limits

And learning to say "no" without any gimmicks

It's about taking care of our bodies and minds

And treating ourselves with compassion and binds

Self-love is a practice, a daily choice
To listen to ourselves, and follow our own voice
It's about taking the time to nurture and heal
And finding our inner strength and zeal

Let us cultivate self-love, with every breath we take
And let us nourish our souls, with every step we make
For when we love ourselves, we inspire others too
And we can create a world that's kinder, for me and
you

"Radiate Positivity"

A positive mindset is a gift

A treasure that you can uplift

A state of mind that opens doors

And helps you to achieve so much more

It starts with the way you think

And the words you choose to speak

With each thought and every word

You shape the life you've always heard

Choose to see the good in all

And let your spirit start to sprawl

With every challenge that you face

You'll find a way to conquer and embrace

Believe in your own strength and power

And let your confidence start to tower

You are capable of amazing things

And the world is yours to spread your wings

Let gratitude be your guide

And let it fill you up inside

With every breath that you take

You'll feel the power of love awake

Be kind to yourself and others too

And let your heart radiate through

For in the light of positivity

You'll find your true creativity

Embrace each moment as it comes

And let your spirit start to hum

With the joy of life's little things

You'll find your inner happiness sings

Cultivate that positive mindset

And let your spirit start to set

The world alight with hope and joy

For you are a shining beacon of light and employ

"Fear of the Future"

Fear of the future, a daunting thought

A fear that can consume and tie us in the knot

The fear of the unknown, what's to come

Can be overwhelming, making us feel numb

What if we fail, what if we fall

What if we can't handle it all

These thoughts and worries, they never end

Anxiety and fear become our only friends

We try to plan, we try to prepare

But the fear of the future is always there

A constant weight, a heavy load

A burden that we struggle to withhold

But what if we could see the future with new eyes

And embrace the uncertainty, without any lies

What if we could trust in ourselves and our strength

And let go of the fear that's of such great length

For the future is not something to be feared

But rather an adventure to be steered

It's a path we walk, a journey we take

And with each step forward, we can create

We can create a life that's full of joy

A life that's free from worry and employed

We can choose to take risks, and embrace the
unknown

And trust in ourselves, to find our own

We may stumble, we may fall

But we have the strength to overcome it all

The fear of the future may still linger

But we can choose to let go, and let it wither

So let's take a step forward, and face the fear

And let go of the worry that's so near

For the future is ours, to embrace and create

And with each step forward, we can appreciate

The beauty of the unknown, the wonder that lies
ahead
The adventures and experiences that will be led
So let go of your fear, and take a leap of faith
And the future will become, a beautiful wraith

The fear of the future may never completely fade
But we have the power to not let it invade
We can embrace the uncertainty and the change
And live a life that's beautiful and strange

"Power of Acceptance"

Accept the person that you are

For all your flaws, both big and small

Accept the things you cannot change

And learn to love yourself through it all

Accept the past, and all that's been

The hurt, the pain, the heartache within

Accept the lessons learned, the growth, the gain

And let them guide you towards your next win

Accept the present, just as it is

The good, the bad, the in-between

Accept the people In your life

And all the love and support they bring

Accept the future, still unknown

And all the possibilities it holds

Accept the challenges, the highs, the lows

And the adventures yet to unfold

Accept the world, with all its flaws

And all the beauty that it shows

Accept the differences, the diversity

And the things that make us grow

Acceptance is a journey, not a destination

A practice to be embraced every day

It's about finding peace within yourself

And in the world, come what may

Accept yourself, and all that's around

For it's in acceptance, that true happiness is found

And in the end, you'll see it's true

Acceptance is the key, to a life that's good and true

"Love and Hate"

Love and hate, two sides of a coin

Inextricably linked, yet so often alone

Love, the warm embrace of the heart

Hate, the icy grip that tears us apart

Love, the feeling that makes us whole

Hate, the anger that takes its toll

Love, the light that guides us through

Hate, the darkness that clouds our view

Love, the sweet melody that sings

Hate, the bitter note that stings

Love, the gentle touch of a hand

Hate, the force that makes us stand

Love, the flower that blooms in the sun

Hate, the thorn that pierces us one by one

Love, the comfort that soothes our soul

Hate, the torment that takes its toll

Love, the joy that fills our heart
Hate, the pain that tears us apart
Love, the bond that connects us all
Hate, the division that makes us fall

Love and hate, they dance and sway
In a never-ending cycle, day by day
But in the end, it's love that will prevail
For it's the only thing that can never fail

Let love be your guide and your light
And hate will fade into the night
For love is the key to a life well-lived
And it's the only thing that can truly give

Love and hate, two sides of a coin
But love is the side that will always win
So embrace love and let it lead the way
And hate will have no power to sway

"Loving Yourself First"

Loving yourself first is not always an easy task

It takes courage, resilience, and a willingness to bask

In the glow of self-love, and the warmth it can bring

To embrace all of who you are, and to let your spirit

sing

It's about accepting yourself, flaws and all

And understanding that perfection is an unrealistic call

It's about knowing your worth, and treating yourself

with care

To prioritize your needs, and the love that you share

It's a journey that starts with self-awareness and

reflection

To examine your beliefs, and challenge your

perception

Of who you are, and what you deserve

To break free from self-doubt, and the fear of being observed

It's about setting boundaries, and learning to say no
To protect your energy, and allow your light to glow
It's about taking care of your mind, body, and soul
To nurture your inner child, and make yourself whole

It's about celebrating your strengths, and your unique traits
To embrace your quirks, and the qualities that make you great
It's about forgiving yourself, for the mistakes you've made
To release the guilt and shame, and let self-love pervade

It's about choosing happiness, and the joy that it brings
To live in the moment, and let your heart take wings
It's about being true to yourself, and living authentically

To let your light shine, and radiate your positivity

Love yourself first, and the rest will fall into place

Trust in your journey, and the power of your own grace

For the love you give to yourself, is the love you attract

And with self-love as your foundation, you can conquer

any act

"The Freedom of Letting Go"

The weight we carry on our shoulders

The burdens we cannot shake

Can drag us down and hold us back

Until we feel we cannot break

But there is a freedom in letting go

Of the things that we cannot control

A release of the tension and the stress

A surrendering of the soul

Letting go can be so difficult

And it may take time to heal

But with each small step we take

We start to feel what's real

We learn to trust the journey

And to have faith in what will be

To let go of the things we can't change

And to set our spirits free

For when we loosen our grip

On the things that weigh us down

We open up space for new beginnings

And joy that knows no bounds

So let go of the past that haunts you

And the fears that hold you tight

Embrace the freedom of letting go

And step into the light

"Path to Inner Peace"

The path to inner peace is a journey we all must take

It's a path that's often long and winding, but it's not fake

It's a journey that starts with a single step

And it's a journey that never really ends, but we keep

It's a journey of self-discovery, of finding ourselves

And it's a journey of healing, of mending our broken shelves

It's about letting go of the past, and living in the present

And it's about finding the beauty in life, that's quite decent

It's a journey of self-love, of accepting ourselves as we are

And it's a journey of self-care, of taking care of our mind and our star

It's about finding our inner voice, and listening to its
wisdom
And it's about trusting ourselves, and our inner
freedom

The path to inner peace is also about letting go of fear
And it's about finding the courage to face life, crystal
clear
It's about finding the strength to face our challenges,
with hope
And it's about finding the faith to cope, with love that's
scope

It's about finding our purpose in life, and living it true
And it's about finding the joy in life, in everything we
do
It's about finding the balance in life, between work and
play
And it's about finding the peace in life, that's here to
stay

The path to inner peace is different for everyone

And it's a journey that's often hard, but never undone

It's a journey that's worth it, in every single way

And it's a journey that leads us to a better day

Let us walk the path to inner peace, with an open heart

And let us trust the journey, from the very start

For in the end, we will find our way

And we will be at peace, each and every day

"The Present Moment Flow"

In the present moment, there's a flow

A rhythm that guides us, wherever we go

It's a gentle current, that carries us along

And helps us find our way, to where we belong

It's easy to get lost in our thoughts

To be pulled by the past, and what it's wrought

Or to be consumed by the future, and what's to come

But in the present moment, is where we must become

For it's in the present moment, that we truly live

Where we can embrace all that life has to give

It's where we can find peace, and let go of strife

And discover the beauty, in the simple things of life

In the present moment, there's a magic that abounds

A beauty that surrounds us, and a love that resounds

It's where we can feel the breeze, upon our face

And let our worries and troubles, be replaced

By the gentle flow, of the present moment stream
That carries us through life, like a peaceful dream
It's a flow that can calm our minds, and ease our pain
And allow us to find the joy, we've searched for in vain

But staying present, can be easier said than done
With distractions and worries, we often succumb
But if we can learn to quiet our minds
And tune into the present moment, we'll find

That the flow is always there, waiting for us to see
To let it guide us, and set our hearts free
For in the present moment, there's a wisdom that's
deep
A knowing that guides us, and helps us to keep

Our focus on what matters, and what truly counts
And to let go of what holds us back, and what mounts

It's where we can find the strength, to face any
challenge
And let our inner light, shine through and manage

Let us embrace the present moment flow
And let it guide us to where we need to go
Let us trust in its wisdom, and let it be our guide
As we journey through life, side by side

For in the present moment, there's a flow that's true
A rhythm that guides us, to be our best self too
It's where we can find the peace, we've been searching
for
And let the beauty of life, become our true score

Let us stay present, and feel the rhythm of the flow
And let the present moment, be our truest glow
For in its magic and beauty, we'll find all that we need
To live a life of purpose, joy, and unbridled feed

"Letting Go"

In life, we hold onto things so tight

Our fears, our worries, our doubts, our might

We cling to what's familiar and known

And fear the future that's yet to be shown

Sometimes we must learn to let go

Of the things that weigh us down below

For in the release we find our might

And our spirits take flight like birds in flight

Let go of the past that's gone and done

And embrace the present that's just begun

Let go of the hurts and pains of old

And find the healing that makes you whole

Let go of the things that cause you stress

And find the peace that brings happiness

Let go of the fear that holds you back

And find the courage to stay on track

For in the act of letting go
We find the strength that we didn't know
We learn to trust in ourselves and more
And find the path that leads to the shore

Let go of the things that hold you down
And find the freedom that comes around
For in the release we find our might
And our spirits take flight like birds in flight

"Banishing Self-Doubt"

Self-doubt, it creeps in like a thief in the night

Stealing away our confidence and our might

It whispers in our ear, like a serpent's hiss

Telling us we're not enough, that we'll never make it to

bliss

We second-guess ourselves, and our abilities

Questioning every decision, and all our possibilities

We become paralyzed, by the fear of failure

And lose sight of our dreams, our passion and our vigor

Self-doubt, it can be a relentless foe

Holding us back, from all that we could sow

It keeps us from taking risks, and stepping out of our

comfort zone

And we stay stagnant, in a place we've long outgrown

But what if we chose, to face our self-doubt head on

To challenge the lies, that we've come to rely upon

To believe in ourselves, and all that we can achieve

And let go of the fears, that we've allowed to deceive

We can choose to focus, on our strengths and our gifts

And not let our weaknesses, become the focal rifts

To remind ourselves, of all that we have accomplished

And not let our self-doubt, leave us feeling astonished

We can learn to embrace, the unknown and the new

And trust in ourselves, that we'll see it through

To silence the doubts, and the inner critic's voice

And replace it with self-love, and a newfound rejoice

Self-doubt, it may always be there

But we can choose how much, we'll let it impair

We can find the courage, to face it with grace

And find our inner strength, in the challenges we face

Let's banish the self-doubt, that's held us back for so
long

And let our inner light, shine forth like a song

For we are capable, of greatness and more

And we won't let self-doubt, hold us back anymore

"Forgive"

Forgiveness is a powerful force

A choice that can redirect life's course

It's not always easy to do

But it's necessary to see things anew

To forgive is to release

To let go of pain that doesn't cease

It's a gift that you give to yourself

To put your heart back on the shelf

When you forgive, you free your soul

From the hurt that once took control

You open yourself to love and light

And you learn to let go of the fight

Forgiveness doesn't mean forgetting

Or pretending that things aren't upsetting

It's a conscious decision to move on

And let the past be forever gone

To forgive is to find peace

To let go of pain and negative release

It's a choice to see the good

And not to dwell on what has stood

Forgiveness is a journey to heal

To let your heart start to feel

It's a way to find your inner grace

And leave behind the past's dark space

To forgive is to be kind

To yourself and those you've left behind

It's a chance to start anew

And to find a way to be true

Forgiveness is a hard road

But it's a journey that we all must tow

It's the key to living free

And finding joy and harmony

Let's take a step towards forgiving

And let your heart start living

It's not an easy thing to do

But it's the kindest gift to give to you

"Miracle of Self-Acceptance"

Self-acceptance is a miracle

A gift we can give ourselves each day

It's about loving ourselves, just as we are

And seeing our worth, in every single way

It's about embracing our strengths and our flaws

And recognizing the beauty in them all

It's about forgiving ourselves for mistakes we've made

And learning to get up after we fall

Self-acceptance is a journey

One that can be bumpy, and winding too

But it's a journey that's worth taking

For the happiness and peace it can imbue

It's about letting go of the need to be perfect

And recognizing our imperfections with love

It's about being kind to ourselves and others

And treating ourselves with the same compassion

we're fond of

Self-acceptance is a journey inward

A journey towards our truest selves

It's about embracing all parts of who we are

And letting our hearts shine bright like wealth

Let us embrace the miracle of self-acceptance

And celebrate the beauty within

For it's in this acceptance of ourselves

That true joy and peace can begin

"Finding Beauty in Imperfection"

In a world obsessed with perfection

It's easy to feel flawed and incomplete

We're taught to hide our imperfections

And strive for an unattainable feat

But what if we learned to embrace our flaws

And see the beauty in imperfection

What if we let go of the need to be perfect

And started to accept ourselves with affection

For imperfection is what makes us unique

It's what sets us apart from the rest

It's a reminder that we're all human

And we're doing our best

So let us find beauty in our imperfections

And celebrate our quirks and flaws

For it's in these imperfections

That our true beauty lies, without pause

Let us learn to love our scars

And see them as a symbol of strength

Let us embrace our mistakes

And learn from them, no matter the length

For finding beauty in imperfection

Is a journey toward self-love

It's a way to accept ourselves

And see ourselves as enough

Let us find beauty in imperfection

And see ourselves in a new light

For it's in embracing our imperfections

That we can truly shine bright

"Tears"

Tears, they flow from deep inside

The well of emotions that we cannot hide

They come in moments of joy and pain

And are a testament to the heart's refrain

Tears, they fall like gentle rain

A release of the soul's deepest pain

They wash away our hurt and fears

And help us to move beyond our tears

Tears, they speak a language of their own

A message from the heart that's shown

They are a reminder that we're alive

And that we're human and we thrive

Tears, they're a sign of our humanity

A symbol of our capacity for empathy

They help us to connect and to relate

And to feel the love that we create

Tears, they hold the memories we keep

Of all the moments we've lived so deep

They tell the story of our lives

And remind us that we will survive

Tears, they can be a source of strength

A way to move beyond the length

They are the healing balm we need

To help us on our journey to succeed

Tears, they are a part of who we are

A reminder that we've come so far

They show the depth of our soul

And the beauty of being whole

Let the tears fall when they may

And know that they will light the way

For they are a testament to life

And a reminder that we will survive

"The Art of Mindfulness"

Mindfulness is an art, a way of life

A practice to keep us in the present moment

It's about being aware of our thoughts and feelings

And accepting them without judgment

It's about paying attention to our breath

And feeling the rise and fall of our chest

It's about noticing the world around us

And being fully present in each moment, at our best

Mindfulness can help us find calm

In the midst of chaos and stress

It can help us appreciate the beauty of life

And see the world with a new, fresh impress

It's about letting go of the past

And not worrying about the future ahead

It's about being here, right now

And living in the moment instead

Mindfulness is a practice we can do
Anytime, anywhere, and anyplace
It's about slowing down, taking a breath
And connecting with our inner grace

Let us practice the art of mindfulness
And find peace within our minds and hearts
For it's in this state of awareness and presence
That we can make a fresh new start

"The Courage to be Vulnerable"

To be vulnerable takes courage and strength

It's about showing our true selves, without pretense or

length

It's about opening up, and revealing our hearts

And taking a risk, even when it's hard and parts

For vulnerability is often seen as a weakness

A flaw to be hidden, and kept under meekness

But the truth is, it's a sign of immense courage

To show our true selves, and let down our walls, in

front and backstage

It's about facing our fears and insecurities

And letting others see us for who we truly be

It's about being honest, and showing our scars

And letting our emotions shine like stars

For it's in our vulnerability, we find connection

With others who understand our pain and affection

It's a way to break down barriers, and find support

And to be seen, heard, and loved, without the retort

Let us have the courage to be vulnerable

And show our true selves, without fear or trouble

For it's in our vulnerability, we find strength and growth

And a way to live life to the fullest, with faith and hope

"Trusting Yourself"

Trust yourself, dear young women, you know what's best
Believe in your instincts, and let them guide you, with no jest
For you have the wisdom and power within
To make the right choices, and begin your own win

It's about listening to your heart and intuition
And trusting your gut, without hesitation or suspicion
It's about knowing your worth and your voice
And making choices that align with your values and rejoice

For sometimes, the world may try to dim your light
And tell you what to do, and what's wrong and right
But don't forget, you have the power within
To make your own choices, and let your own light shine and grin

Trust yourself, and don't be afraid to take a chance

And follow your dreams, even if it may seem like a trance

For life is too short to play it safe and small

Trust yourself, and take that leap, and stand tall

For you are strong, and brave, and full of light

And the world needs your voice, and your might

Trust yourself, dear young women, and know

That you have what it takes, to let your own beauty show

"Releasing the Past"

The past can be a heavy weight to bear

A burden that we carry, a cross we must wear

The memories that haunt us, the pain we endure

It can be hard to let go, to find a cure

But holding on to what's already gone

Will only bring us down, and keep us undone

For the past is over, it's done and gone

And dwelling on it, will only prolong

The hurt and the anger, the resentment and pain

Are emotions that keep us trapped, in a cycle of disdain

It's time to let go, to find forgiveness and peace

And to find a new way, to make the hurt cease

To release the past, is to set ourselves free

To move on from what was, and to find what can be

It's about forgiveness, of ourselves and of others

And finding the strength, to let go of the druthers

For in releasing the past, we make room for the present

We find a new way, to be more pleasant

To embrace the lessons, that the past has taught

And to use them to grow, and to find our own lot

Let us release the past, and find our peace

And let go of the hurt, and the memories that cease

For it's in letting go, that we find our power

And the strength to move forward, and find our own flower

"Embracing Change"

Change is an inevitable part of life

A constant ebb and flow, amidst both joy and strife

It can be scary, daunting, and bring forth unease

As we grapple with new paths, and things we cannot

foresee

It takes courage to face change, to let go of the old

To trust in the journey, and have faith to unfold

To let go of what was, and open up to what could be

And find new ways to live, and set ourselves free

Sometimes change is forced upon us, and we have no

choice

While other times we seek it, to discover our inner

voice

Regardless of how it comes, we must embrace it all the

same

For it's a natural part of life, and to resist is to suffer in
vain

We may resist and cling, to what we know so well
But when we embrace change, we can break free from
our shell
We can see with new eyes, and discover fresh
perspectives
And find new joy and peace, as we embark on new
directives

It's not easy to let go, to surrender and release
To face the unknown, and the fear that it may unleash
But when we embrace change, with an open heart and
mind
We can find new possibilities, and leave our fears
behind

Let us welcome change, with open arms and grace
To let it unfold, and reveal a new face

For when we embrace change, we can watch our lives unfold

And discover new adventures, as our story is told

"The Power of Forgiveness"

Forgiveness is a powerful tool

A way to heal wounds and to break through

It takes courage and strength to forgive

But it's the only way to truly live

For holding onto anger and pain

Will only bring us more of the same

It's like a weight that drags us down

And keeps us stuck, unable to move around

But with forgiveness, we can break free

From the chains of anger and misery

We can find peace and clarity of mind

And leave the past, far behind

Forgiveness is not about forgetting

It's about accepting and letting

It's about acknowledging what has been

And choosing to release it, from deep within

It's about healing the wounds that we carry
And finding the strength to not be wary
It's about seeing the good in all
And not allowing the hurt, to make us fall

For forgiveness is a gift we give ourselves
A way to find peace, amongst the chaos and bells
It's a way to find our inner strength
And to live life, to its fullest length

So let us embrace the power of forgiveness
And let go of the pain and the distress
For in forgiving, we find our power
And the strength to bloom, like a flower

"Celebrating Unique Spirit"

We all have a spirit, that is uniquely our own

A spark that ignites, and guides us to be known

It's what makes us different, and sets us apart

And it's a beauty, that should be celebrated from the

start

For our unique spirit, is what makes us shine

It's what makes us special, one of a kind

It's a reflection of who we truly are

And it's a reminder, to always follow our own star

Let us celebrate, our unique spirit within

Embrace our differences, and let our true selves begin

For it's in celebrating, our unique spirit and light

That we can make the world, a more beautiful sight

Let us not be afraid, to be who we truly are

And to let our unique spirit, shine bright like a star

For it's in celebrating, the beauty of diversity

That we can find true harmony, and unity

Embrace your unique spirit, and let it lead the way

For it's in following it, that we find our own path to
sway

And let us celebrate, the unique spirit of others too

For together, we can create a world, that's vibrant and
anew

"Cultivating Inner Joy"

Happiness, contentment, and inner joy

Are the treasures we seek, as we journey through life's

plow

We search for meaning, and purpose in our existence,

And strive to find peace, in a world of resistance

But inner joy isn't something that can be found

It's something that grows, from within the ground

It's a seed that we plant, and nurture with care

And with time and patience, it will surely bear

It starts with the present, and being in the now

To find joy in small things, and learn to take a bow

To cherish each moment, and embrace all that's new

To live life fully, and find the joy that's in you

It's learning to appreciate, the beauty of life

To find gratitude, amidst all the strife

To live with purpose, and do what you love

And to find inner peace, like a soaring dove

Cultivating inner joy, is a daily practice

A journey inward, to a place of pure bliss

It's finding the light, that shines from within

And letting it guide you, through thick and thin

So take a deep breath, and let it all go

Open your heart, and let your spirit glow

Find joy in the journey, and in every step you take

And let the light of inner joy, be your constant wake

"Overcoming Self-Doubt"

The whispers of self-doubt can be deafening

A voice that echoes, relentlessly, unrelenting

It tells us we're not enough, that we're not worthy

That we'll never succeed, and our dreams are too lofty

It feeds on our insecurities, and takes root in our mind

And the more we listen, the harder it is to unwind

It's a battle we fight, every day of our lives

To silence the doubts, and let our spirit thrive

But the truth is, we are more than our doubts

We're capable of greatness, of breaking through the clouds

We have the strength and resilience, to overcome our fears

To rise above the noise, and wipe away the tears

It starts with believing in ourselves, and our worth

To know that we're enough, and have been since birth

To celebrate our strengths, and accept our flaws

And to trust in our journey, despite its unknowns

We must learn to reframe, the way we see ourselves

To focus on our potential, and not on our shells

To be kind to ourselves, and treat ourselves with care

To love and accept ourselves, just as we are

And when self-doubt comes knocking, as it often will

We can stand our ground, and refuse to give it any thrill

We can remind ourselves of our worth, and our strength

And keep moving forward, one step at a time, no matter the length

For overcoming self-doubt, is a journey worth taking

A chance to break free, and find our own awakening

It's a process of growth, and a discovery of self

And with each victory, we gain more confidence and wealth

"Finding Grace in the Storm"

In the midst of chaos, it's easy to feel lost

As the winds of change and uncertainty toss

You around and around, in a sea of confusion

But hold on, my dear, for there's a solution

Amidst the storm, there lies a hidden grace

A calmness that you can embrace

A light that shines even in the darkest night

A guide that leads you towards the light

It's the stillness that's found within

The peace that you can always begin

To cultivate and nurture every day

To find your way and pave your own way

It's the acceptance of what is

Without resistance, without any whiz

To let go of what you can't control

And find solace in the serenity of your soul

It's the faith that you hold deep inside

The trust that everything will be alright

The belief that you're strong enough to endure

And that every challenge is a chance to mature

When the storm clouds gather above

And the thunder rumbles with all its might

Take a deep breath and find your center

For within you, there's a grace that's always bright

"Finding Light in the Darkness"

When the darkness surrounds us

And we can't see the light

We may feel lost and hopeless

With no end in sight

But within the darkness

There is always a spark

A glimmer of hope and courage

That can light up the dark

It may be a small flame

But it's enough to guide the way

To help us find our footing

And face the challenges of the day

Look within yourself

And find that light within

Let it guide you through the darkness

And help you find your grin

For though the night may seem endless

And the shadows may be deep

There is always a ray of light

That can help us rise and leap

And when the morning comes

And the light breaks through the night

We'll be stronger and more resilient

For having found our own inner light

"The Gift of Mindful Presence"

In this chaotic world we live in
We're always rushing here and there
Our minds a flurry of activity
And we forget to just be aware

But there is a gift in mindful presence
A way to slow down and connect
To the present moment and to ourselves
And to let our spirits intersect

With mindful presence we're fully here
In body, mind, and soul
We notice the world around us
And we feel more whole

We savor every breath we take
And each moment that we're given
We're grateful for the simple things

And the beauty that surrounds us, even

We become more attuned to our needs
And the needs of those we love
We listen more deeply to our hearts
And to the wisdom from above

The gift of mindful presence
Is a treasure that we can't deny
For it brings us peace and clarity
And a sense of being fully alive

Let us strive to be present
In each moment of our day
And may the gift of mindful presence
Guide us in every single way

"The Healing Power of Nature"

Amidst the chaos of our daily lives

Nature remains a calming force

Its healing power, a balm for our souls

A source of peace and of course

Whether it's the rustling of leaves

Or the sound of waves crashing on the shore

The beauty of a vibrant sunset

Or the awe-inspiring grandeur of a mountain range to

explore

Nature holds a special place

In our hearts and in our minds

It reminds us of the majesty of life

And helps us leave our cares behind

In the midst of our hectic days

A walk in nature can bring clarity

As we breathe in the fresh air

And let our minds roam free

With each step we take on the trail

We feel our spirits come alive

As we connect with the beauty around us

And feel gratitude for being alive

The healing power of nature

Is something we can all embrace

For in its midst, we find respite

And a renewed sense of grace

Let us take the time we need

To immerse ourselves in the natural world

And in its presence, may we find

The healing that we need to unfurl

"Gratitude for the Present"

In a world where we're always striving

For the next big thing, the newest gadget

It's easy to lose sight of what we have

And take the present for granted

But if we pause and take a moment

To reflect on what we do possess

We may be surprised to find

That we're already truly blessed

For in this moment, right now

We have the gift of life

We have the breath in our lungs

And the beating of our heart, rife

We have the love of those around us

And the beauty of the world to behold

We have the opportunity to create

To learn, to grow, to be bold

Let us take a moment
To express gratitude for the present
For all the joys and blessings
That this moment represents

Let us cherish what we have
And the opportunities before us
For in the present lies the power
To create a life that truly thrills us

So as we journey through this life
Let us never lose sight
Of the blessings that we have right now
And the present's wondrous light

"Learning to Live Fearlessly"

There is a life beyond the fear

A path that leads to freedom clear

To live with courage, without dread

To face the unknown, with a steady head

It starts with a simple step

A decision made to leave regrets

To live in the moment, not in the past

To embrace the future, and make it last

It takes strength to overcome our fears

To rise above, and wipe away the tears

To trust ourselves, and take a chance

To open our hearts, and learn to dance

With every step, we grow stronger

With every breath, we last longer

Our courage shines like a blazing sun

Our fear diminished, and overcome

So take that step, with head held high
Embrace the fear, and let it fly
For in its place, love will grow
And fearlessness will start to show

And when we learn to live this way
Our lives are filled with joy each day
Let us live fearlessly, with all our might
And embrace the world, with pure delight

"The Serenity of Surrender"

In life's journey, there comes a time
When we face challenges that seem impossible to
climb
We hold on tight to what we know
But sometimes it's best to let go

For in the act of surrendering
We find a sense of serenity that's so liberating
It's like a weight being lifted off our chest
As we allow life to take care of the rest

Surrender doesn't mean giving up the fight
But rather, it's choosing to see the light
And trusting that everything will be alright
Even when the path ahead is not in sight

It takes courage to let go of control
To release the fears that grip our soul

But when we surrender, we open the door

To a world of possibilities we never saw before

We learn to embrace the present moment

Without the burden of the past or the worry of what's

to come

And in that stillness, we find a peace so profound

That can only be experienced when we surrender and

let go all around

Let us surrender to the ebb and flow of life

And trust that we'll come out of the storm alright

For in the serenity of surrender, we find our way

To a brighter tomorrow, one step at a time, each day

"The Joy of Simple Pleasures"

The world may seem chaotic and loud

A place where peace is hard to be found

But amidst the hustle and bustle of life

There are moments of bliss that ease our strife

The joy of simple pleasures, oh how sweet

The little things in life that make us complete

The taste of warm coffee on a chilly day

A soothing bath at night to wash our cares away

A walk in the park on a sunny afternoon

Watching the sunset, a glorious boon

A good book that takes us to another world

Or a quiet moment with our beloved pet, curled

The laughter of children, pure and carefree

The embrace of a loved one, a sense of security

A home-cooked meal that fills our heart and soul

A meaningful conversation that makes us whole

These simple pleasures may seem small

But they have the power to heal us all

In times of stress and anxiety

We must remember to seek out serenity

Let us find joy in the little things

And the peace that they bring

For in the midst of life's uncertainty

The simple pleasures can set us free

"Cultivating a Heart of Gratitude"

Open your eyes to the world around

And see the beauty that surrounds

The sun that rises in the sky

And the clouds that dance on high

The chirping of the morning birds

And the rustling of the leaves unheard

The flowers that bloom in the fields

And the fragrance that the breeze yields

Embrace the moments that make you smile

And be grateful for every mile

That you have traveled on your journey

And all the lessons that you've learned

For every person that has touched your life

And every challenge that you have survived

For every gift that you have received

And every moment of grace you believed

Let your heart overflow with gratitude

For the blessings that you have accrued

And the love that surrounds you every day

Let gratitude be the path you choose to pave

For in gratitude, we find the light

That guides us through the darkest night

And with a heart that's full of grace

We can conquer any obstacle we face

"The Miracle of Self-Compassion"

Sometimes we are our harshest critic

Judging ourselves for every flaw and misstep

We berate ourselves for every mistake

As if we must be perfect to be acceptable

But in truth, this is a fallacy

A myth that we tell ourselves to maintain control

For in reality, self-compassion is the key

To unlock our true potential and living whole

Self-compassion is the gentle voice

That speaks kindly to our wounded hearts

It helps us to see that we have a choice

To heal ourselves and make a fresh start

It is the recognition that we are human

And that perfection is an impossible feat

It is the acceptance of our imperfections

And the realization that they make us complete

When we practice self-compassion

We learn to forgive ourselves and let go

We begin to see the beauty in our imperfections

And we discover a newfound glow

Let us be kind to ourselves

And show ourselves the love we deserve

For in doing so, we will find a greater wealth

And a life that is rich and well-preserved

"Magic of Mindful Living"

In a world that moves so fast

We often forget to take a breath and last

We rush through life without much thought

Failing to realize the things that we have sought

The magic of mindful living is in the present

Taking a moment to pause and be observant

Noticing the world around us, the sights and sounds

Being fully present in the moments that astound

It's about slowing down and being intentional

And finding beauty in the things that are

unconventional

The simple things that we often overlook

But in reality, they deserve a second look

The beauty of a sunset, the sound of the rain

The way the leaves dance in the wind again and again

The warmth of a hug, the taste of a favorite meal

The small things that make life so real

It's about finding joy in the mundane

And realizing that each moment is not in vain

Being grateful for what we have and who we are

And accepting ourselves just as we are

The magic of mindful living is in the now

Taking a deep breath and allowing it to flow

It's about living life with intention and purpose

And finding peace in the present, in every moment

that surfaces

"Grace of Letting Your Heart Lead"

Oh, the grace that comes

From letting your heart lead

The way it beats with passion

A force that cannot be misread

For too long you've silenced

The voice that speaks within

But now you realize it's power

And how it guides you from within

No longer bound by fear

Or swayed by other's will

Your heart, the compass, leads you

And you feel the world stand still

It's in those quiet moments

Where you sit and simply be

That you feel the magic happen

And the grace of life you see

With each breath that you take
You feel your heart expand
And all the joy and peace
You'd hoped for now at hand

Embrace the grace of letting go
And let your heart take flight
For it will guide you to your dreams
And everything will be alright

"Wisdom of Self-Love"

In this world of chaos and strife

We often forget the beauty of life

We chase our dreams and work so hard

Forgetting to give ourselves a loving regard

We often think we're not enough

That we must be perfect, smooth and tough

We strive to fit in with societal norms

Ignoring the voice inside that warns

But dear friend, you must know

That loving yourself is the way to go

It's the foundation of a happy life

The cornerstone of all joy and strife

Self-love is not a selfish act

It's a necessity that we often lack

It's the seed of all that we can be

The key to living peacefully and free

So, take a moment to reflect and see

The beauty that lies within thee

Embrace yourself with open arms

And let self-love work its charms

It's not an easy path to take

But it's worth it for your own sake

So, be gentle, kind and true

And let the wisdom of self-love guide you

"Power of Positive Self-Talk"

In the depths of our minds

Lies a voice that we oftentimes find

Whispering doubts and fears

That hold us back from facing our fears

But what if we could change that tone

And speak to ourselves in a different known?

What if we could use positive self-talk

To uplift our spirits and break the lock?

We have the power to shape our thoughts

And steer our minds towards positive knots

With each word we say

We can guide our hearts towards a brighter day

When we feel low and down

Let's replace our inner critic's frown

With words of encouragement and support

That will help us persevere and not fall short

So let's speak to ourselves with love and kindness

And leave behind our inner critic's blindness

With positive self-talk, we can break free

And unlock the doors to the best version of you and

me

"Joy of Loving Yourself"

In a world that often seems to demand

Perfection, success, and unattainable standards

We can get lost in the noise and the chaos

Forgetting the beauty and power within us

But there is a way to rise above the fray

To find a sense of peace and joy each day

And it all begins with the simple act

Of loving yourself, as you are, in fact

This love is not a shallow or fleeting thing

But a deep and abiding self-understanding

It is knowing your worth and your potential

And recognizing the strengths that are essential

It is accepting your flaws and imperfections

And treating yourself with kindness and affection

It is choosing to see the good in yourself

And letting go of the doubts that can bring you down

When you love yourself, you open the door

To a world of possibilities and so much more

You can soar to new heights and achieve your dreams

And find the strength to weather life's storms, it seems

Embrace the joy of loving yourself

And let your heart be your guide and your wealth

For in this love, you'll find the key

To a life of fulfillment and possibility

"Finding Clarity in Confusion"

In the midst of confusion, it's hard to see

The path we should take, the way we should be

Our minds are clouded, our thoughts all a mess

And the more we struggle, the more we feel distress

But amidst the chaos, there is a light

A glimmer of hope, shining ever so bright

It's the clarity we seek, the peace we desire

And it's waiting for us, if we're willing to aspire

We must be still and listen to our hearts

Let go of our fears, and any doubts that impart

For in the stillness, we will find our way

To the truth that will guide us each and every day

Sometimes we must surrender and let go

Of the things we can't control, and the things we know

For it's in the surrender that we find the power

To move forward with courage, and to flower

Through the confusion, we must keep the faith
That everything happens for a reason, and it's not too
late
To find our purpose, our passion, and our voice
And to make choices that will help us rejoice

So, let us embrace the confusion and the unknown
And trust that the seeds we've sown
Will bring forth the clarity and the peace we seek
And help us live our lives full and complete

"Strength of Your Spirit"

In the midst of the chaos and turmoil

When the world seems to have lost its coil

And your heart is heavy with fear and doubt

Remember the strength of your spirit, never to be

without

The winds of change may blow you away

But the roots of your spirit will always stay

Deep within, anchoring you to the ground

A firm foundation for you to rebound

The road ahead may be steep and rough

With many obstacles and challenges enough

But trust in the power of your inner light

To guide you through even the darkest night

Let go of the doubts and the fears that bind

And allow your spirit to shine and unwind

Embrace your true self with open arms

And let your spirit soar and work its charms

For within you lies an unbreakable force

A source of strength, courage, and remorse

The power of your spirit, bright and true

A light that will guide you through and through

"Strength of Your Inner Compassion"

In the depths of your heart lies a powerful force

That can guide you through life's most difficult course

It's the strength of your inner compassion

That can bring you comfort and satisfaction

It's easy to get lost in the chaos of the world

To be pulled and pushed, and feel like you're swirled

But when you tap into your inner well of grace

You can find the calm in any stormy space

Compassion is a powerful tool in your kit

It helps you to see through the fog and mist

It allows you to open your heart to others

And to see the world from a perspective that's not just

yours

When you treat yourself with kindness and care

You invite compassion to grow and flourish there

It becomes a beacon that guides you in the dark
And it helps you to find your way when you're lost in
the park

Compassion isn't just about how you treat yourself
It's about how you show up for others as well
It's about listening with an open heart and mind
And about being present, and not leaving anyone
behind

Compassion is a practice that you can cultivate
It's about acknowledging the suffering of others, both
small and great
It's about being willing to lend a helping hand
And about seeing the beauty in every woman and man

When you live with compassion, you'll find that your
world shifts
That your heart becomes lighter, and your spirit lifts
You'll find joy in the simplest things, like the sun and
the rain

And you'll see that the world is full of love and not pain

Compassion isn't just about what you do or say
It's about how you show up in the world each day
It's about being true to your values and beliefs
And about living a life that's authentic and free

So cultivate the strength of your inner compassion
And let it guide you through life's twists and turns with passion
Remember that it's a powerful force that can heal
And that it's the foundation for a life that's truly real

For when you live with compassion, you'll find that you're strong
That you can conquer anything, and that you belong
You'll find that you're capable of living your dreams
And that you're a beautiful, radiant, and powerful being

"Letting Your Light Shine"

Letting your light shine, oh how it glows

A beacon of hope, wherever you go

It's the radiance that comes from within

A reflection of the goodness that resides in

There's a power that dwells deep inside

A light that cannot be dimmed or denied

It's the essence of who you truly are

And it's time to let it shine, like a shining star

Don't be afraid to let your light glow

For it's the source of the magic that you sow

It's the spark that ignites your soul

And it's the fuel that keeps you whole

Let your light shine, so bright and true

In everything you say, and everything you do

It's the joy that brings warmth to your heart

And it's the courage that sets you apart

In a world that can be dark and cold
Your light shines bright, like pure gold
It's the hope that we all need to see
And it's the love that sets us free

So let your light shine, like a guiding star
A symbol of love, that's traveled so far
It's the light that leads us home
And it's the light that reminds us we're not alone

Embrace your light, with all your might
And let it shine, oh so bright
For it's the gift that you've been given
And it's the light that will keep on living

Let your light shine, let it shine bright
For it's the source of all that's right
It's the beacon that calls us home
And it's the light that we all have known

"Beauty of Being Enough"

In a world that often tells us we're not enough
It's important to embrace ourselves, and all of our stuff
To let go of the comparisons, and societal norms
And find beauty in being who we are, in all forms

For we are unique, with our own talents and gifts
And we have the power to create our own shifts
To love ourselves fully, and believe in our worth
To let go of perfection, and celebrate our quirks

It's not about conforming, to fit a certain mold
But about embracing our individuality, and being bold
To let our light shine, and be true to who we are
To follow our passions, and reach for the stars

For true beauty is not found in the external
But in the way we love ourselves, and keep it internal
It's about accepting our flaws, and embracing our scars

And loving ourselves, just the way we are

Let's not let society dictate, how we should feel
Or let the media's images, make us question what's
real
For we are enough, just as we are
And our beauty shines, like a bright star

Let's embrace our uniqueness, and love ourselves
fiercely
And let go of any doubts, that make us feel queasy
For the beauty of being enough, lies within our soul
And it's a gift that we should treasure, and let it unfold

Let's celebrate ourselves, and all of our strengths
And know that we're enough, no matter what our
length
For we are beautiful, just as we are
And our light shines bright, like a shooting star

Let's embrace our beauty, and let it shine

And love ourselves fully, all of the time

For the beauty of being enough, is a gift to be
cherished

And it's a reminder, that we are all beautifully
nourished

"Thank you, Young Lady"

Thank you, young lady, for being who you are
For lighting up this world, like a shining star
For sharing your talents, your heart, your soul
And for making this world, a much better whole

Thank you, for your kindness, and your empathy
For your courage, and your vulnerability
For standing up for what is right, and just
And for showing love and compassion, without any fuss

Thank you, for your resilience, and your strength
For rising up from challenges, that seemed to great in length
For taking risks, and following your dreams
And for inspiring others, to believe in their own teams

Thank you, for your curiosity, and your thirst for
knowledge
For seeking out truth, and not being afraid to
acknowledge
The complexities of this world, and the issues we face
And for working towards solutions, with grace and with
pace

Thank you, for your creativity, and your imagination
For seeing the world, in a way that's full of inspiration
For expressing yourself, through art, through music,
through dance
And for bringing beauty and joy, into every
circumstance

Thank you, for your friendship, and your support
For being a listening ear, and offering comfort
For sharing laughter, and tears, and all the in-between
And for being there, whenever someone needed to be
seen

Thank you, for your love, and your generosity

For giving of yourself, without expecting reciprocity

For making this world, a kinder and more loving place

And for spreading hope, and joy, and a brighter embrace

Thank you, young lady, for showing us the way

For standing up, and shining bright each day

For being a beacon, of hope and inspiration

And for sharing your light, with such dedication

You have faced challenges, and struggled at times

But you have never let that dim your shine

You have persevered, and grown so strong

And shown us all, where we truly belong

You have taught us about resilience, and inner strength

And about how to find joy, even in moments of length

You have shown us the beauty, of being true to ourselves

And about the power, of embracing our inner wealth

You have reminded us, to be kind and compassionate

To ourselves and to others, without hesitation

To reach out and lift up, those who may be struggling

And to offer our love, without any buffering

You have shown us, the importance of community

And the strength that comes from unity

You have inspired us, to reach for the stars

And to embrace all of life's scars

Thank you, young lady, for all that you do

For being a light, that shines so true

For reminding us, of our own potential

And for making this world, so much more special

May you always know, how much you are loved

And how much your presence, is a gift from above

May you continue to inspire, and shine so bright

And know that you are, a true guiding light

Thank you for reading this collection of my poems. I hope it has brought you comfort ort and inspiration when you encounter difficult times, and hope these words can help you find inner peace and happiness. May these poems remind you that you are strong, capable, and worthy of love and happiness. May these words encourage you to embrace your true self.

with all my love,

Diane Shirewood

Bio:

Meet Diane - a passionate writer, former fashion industry professional, and mother of three who found her true calling in writing. With over 25 years of experience in fashion, Diane now writes about personal growth and development topics, particularly for young adults. She is an expert in mindfulness and has a special interest in helping young people build strong mindsets and develop resilience. Diane's writing is infused with warmth, authenticity, and compassion, making it accessible and relatable for all readers.

Made in United States
Troutdale, OR
01/15/2024

16944877R00089